Melodious Verse

A Collection of Poetry and Verse

Josehf Lloyd Murchison

Order this book online at www.trafford.com
or email orders@trafford.com

Most Trafford titles are also available at major online book retailers.

Printed in the United States of America.

ISBN: 978-1-4907-5017-0 (sc)
ISBN: 978-1-4907-5016-3 (e)

Trafford rev. 11/04/2014

Trafford
PUBLISHING® www.trafford.com
North America & international
toll-free: 1 888 232 4444 (USA & Canada)
fax: 812 355 4082

Authors Biography

Born in Cornwall Ontario Canada my family followed my fathers work construction, to Mississauga and Toronto, Ontario. My father worked on famous sites as the Cornwall Sea Way, the Commerce Court, and the CN Tower.

I sometimes like to say I was born under an oriental curse, "May your life be interesting."

Josehf is Spanish and Aramaic spelling of Joseph, however that is not why my name is spelled with a hf. My parents screwed up the spelling when I was born. When people ask me why I don't change my name to Joseph, I tell them I don't in order to irritate my parents. After all, Why should I change my name to fix their mistake?

An odd story goes with my name, my grandfather was Joseph Lloyd Foubert and I was named after my grandfather. When he discovered the spelling mistake my grandfather kidnapped me and had me baptized Joseph so god would know who I was.

I write short stories and poetry for the love of writing. I started writing over thirty years ago when I was in high school, where I met my wife Mary Anne. We are the proud parents of two sons Joshua and Michael.

May you enjoy reading my writing as much as I enjoyed writing it?

Josehf Lloyd Murchison

Foreword

I never write unless I am inspired. If I write when I'm not inspired the words feel forced into being as if I were talking just to be heard. They carry little emotion to touch the soul or to inspire the mind. Unlike some other poets my poetry is not just ode to my love, a flower or tree. I drift in subject matter, length and style.

I have read poetry books where every poem is the same. Even famous poets have written poetry that can be sung to the same tune throughout the entire book. They sing with the same rhyme, number of paragraphs and tune as if the writer can find none other to sing or write. And after a while all that the reader reads is the same song over and over until they can endure no more and close the book.

When I read or write I like to find something new with each turn of the page. Like the dawning of a new day a new feeling, song or inspiration. The words forming a tapestry in the mind with each stroke of the pen upon the page and a new tapestry with each page turned. Alive and vibrant with a life in words they sing as songbirds in the morning, touching all that hear their melody of emotions in the dawn.

This is poetry, drawing you in as if the words are your lover's arms. Caressing and kissing you in their touch as each emotion becomes a part of you. Every word is a step towards your heart, each paragraph the touching of minds and each poem a part of your soul.

By
Josehf Lloyd Murchison

Love

All but two of my love poems are written to my wife Anne. Part of what has helped us stay together through the hard times has been poetry. Our hearts melded together as one in life.

I
L-O-V-E
Y-O-U

I sit and I listen, to the wind whistle by.
Looking at the light, from the moon in the sky.
I hear the crickets calling, to the stares in the heavens above.
One look into your eyes, I know I am in love.
I kiss you very gently, and hold you in my arms.
Vibrant is your beauty; I love you and your charms.
I walk across the world, with you near my heart.
Even wild horses, could not tear our love apart.
In the morning's light, we walk along the bay.
You feel the waves lapping, and see the waters spray.
I hold your hand gently, and pull you close to me.
Our love it is growing, for all that dare to see.
I wed you in the morrow, I give you true loves kiss.
United we are happy, and will never be remiss.

By
Josehf Lloyd Murchison

My Valentine Anne

No matter where I walk, when we are apart.
You are always near and live within my heart.

My dreams are filled with visions of you.
My love will stand and always be true.

I have traveled this land from coast to coast.
I know it is you that I love the most.

Now I know that this is the time.
Will you be my valentine?

Love Joey

By
Josehf Lloyd Murchison

My love

Some think of her as fat, ugly and grotesque.
Yet she does not feel fat when I hold her in my arms.
She does not look ugly when I gaze upon her face.
She does not seem grotesque when I kiss her.

For I love her.

I can not wait until the day she carries our love within her.
For she is mine within my heart and she will always be with me.

By
Josehf Lloyd Murchison

True Love

I looked into her eyes gently.
I saw her love burning inside.
Her love for me was growing.
As we both stood there and cried.

I'm leaving in the morning.
When I return, I do not know.
I only hope that while I'm gone.
Your love for me will grow.

I returned a while later.
Her love did not stay true.
I found her with another man.
A friend that I once knew.

By
Josehf Lloyd Murchison

Happy Birthday

Throughout the years, you're in my heart.
I dread the times we are apart.
I hope this is just the start.
Happy birthday to you.
My Sweetheart
Love Joey

By
Josehf Lloyd Murchison

Woman

A breast upon her body;
all men they do adore.
When you think they have enough,
they always ask for more.

A breast upon her body;
its pleasure is unbound,
for only in a lover's arms,
their beauty can be found.

A breast upon her body;
all covered laid in silk.
When in time they ripen,
they give you mother's milk.

A breast upon her body;
a beauty to behold.
A pleasure to every man,
whether young or old.

By
Josehf Lloyd Murchison

Life

I wrote this Waka on 9/11 when the Twin Towers fell. In memory of the Firemen that died that day. And the ones that put their lives on the line every day. May their gift of life never be forgotten.

Hero

They carry not a gun or knife.
To save us all they serve their life.

By
Josehf Lloyd Murchison

The Poet

He was a poet young and bright.
He never had fame from the things he did write.
He never was brave or the king of the town.
He just did his own thing, and traveled around.

By
Josehf Lloyd Murchison

Melodious Verse

The sweet joy of emotions lived eternal upon the page.
A moment suspended in time by the muses of a melodious heart,
overflowing with life's winsome passions lived.

Life's woeful sorrows endured, the touch of the morning sun upon ones
face or a lovers kiss upon the lips. The sweet sent of a flower or the
sight of a raptor in flight, the bittersweet tears of a long lost love, made
eternal to be relived upon recitation of verse.

This is Poetry.

By
Josehf Lloyd Murchison

Story Structure

Some writers leave a story at the climax, like an adolescent
male leaving the reader not totally satisfied. Other writers
never bring the reader the climax, of their story.

Good writers take the reader with them. They start the story with an
introduction to the body of characters. Learning every nuance and
curve of each, the writer brings them to life with every stroke of the
pen. Gradually easing the reader into the main body of the story.

Building page, by page, and chapter, after chapter, until the readers
are unable to restrain themselves from turning the next page.

Slowly the reader becomes the main character. Living every
moment, feeling every pleasure, pain, and sorrow as slowly
the reader reaches the climax. Then after the reader is spent,
the writer eases the reader down slowly with the epilog.

Ending the story with the reader in the afterglow of the tale.

By
Josehf Lloyd Murchison

A Noise

A noise from my childhood, well I don't know,
a bird, a sparrow, 'twas so long ago.

A carp when it splashes spawning in the lake.
The roar of a lawnmower, or the swish of a rake.

These are some noises, just a few, which one shale I write about?
I wish I knew.

By
Josehf Lloyd Murchison

Gossamer Carpets in the Spring.

Shimmering lights the color of fire from the early morning sun dance upon gossamer carpets covering fences, trees and grass, the hair of angles covering the world of fields and forest in the spring.

Invisible to the eye, newly born spiders cast out webs like a fisherman casting his net to catch fish, they cast to catch the air and drift upon the currents in the wind to a new home. Far from their place of birth they set down to create a place in the grass to feed on the newborn offspring of the creatures long dead in the fall. Spreading over all the world of meadows and forests alike, creating monuments to aeons of evolution.

Finely spun webs of architectures to numerous to count they set their traps to await the unwary victims of inexperience they feed upon. In time they grow to be formidable predators in a microscopic world of god's creation, creatures so varied and strange in form as to astound the imagination of diversity.

In this world even the predators are prey to the wasp or a sparrow, creatures to feed their young in nests or a hive. Not all succumb to the predators, many live to mate, reproduce and lay eggs to create gossamer carpets in the spring.

By
Josehf Lloyd Murchison

New Day

I sit watching god's creatures of the night,
fleeing from the ever-approaching dawn.
A bright orange and red haze caresses the horizon.
Beyond this is the sun.

Slowly ever so slowly rising above the edge of the earth:
to explode into an orange ball of fire.
Sending a red-river of shimmering light across the water,
now it is dawn.

I can hear the cries of a seagull as it gracefully glides by me.
In the water ducks swim around,
as the sun lights up the world.
It becomes morning,
it is dawn no more,
but a new day.

By
Josehf Lloyd Murchison

Pond

I sit by a pond near a river.
The moon glistening like a river of light.
The crickets call to the lovers.
Walking beneath the stars in the night.

I hear an owl calling to who I do not know.
I see a fire fly flying with a blue green glow.
I build a small fire and play a happy tune.

As I sit there and I listen.
To the call of a single loon.

By
Josehf Lloyd Murchison

Summer in the Park

Under the sky the lovers know.
Long gone the cold of winters snow.
The children's laughter is so gay.
In the sun they sing and play.

On a summer breeze, the flowers blow.
Beneath the sun they spread and grow.
And in the park they spend the day.
Warm breezes chase their cares away.

On the beach they lie in the sun.
And splash in the water just for fun.
Scantly clad they spend the day.
As the hours while away.

By
Josehf Lloyd Murchison

Cats and dogs

What are cats and dogs good for?
To eat the chips that fall on the floor.
The ones we do not eat no more.
Is that what cats and dogs are for?

They cuddle close when we are cold.
A friend to us when we are old.
Chasing mice and acting bold.
Filled with love that is untold.

By
Josehf Lloyd Murchison

Potential

I have the Power to make the world a better place.
I have the Opportunity to make someone's day bright.
I have the Time to make my love happy.
I have the Energy to make a difference.
I have the Nobility to make the downtrodden proud.
I have the Tolerance to make the unlovable loved.
I have the Intelligence to make others see.
I have the Ability to make angels come true.
I have the Love to make our father in heaven shine.
I have the POTENTIAL to make good and not evil.

By
Josehf Lloyd Murchison

My name, Josehf and the poem Pond inspire Spelling. People keep telling me I should change my name from Josehf to Joseph. But the last straw was when someone corrected the spelling in the poem Pond.

Spelling

Please don't correct my spelling.
To me it is a pain.
I tell this to my readers.
Their reaction is the same.

Please don't correct my spelling.
I show you my ID.
It's Josehf not Joseph.
I know just who I be.

Please don't correct my spelling.
I've heard an owls call.
It's who to all that listen.
Not whom I say to all.

Please don't correct my spelling.
To this I loudly cry.
For if no one will listen.
I think that I will die.

By
Josehf Lloyd Murchison

I

I was chosen.
I did not choose.
I can not win.
I will not lose.

I feel pain.
I see the light.
I can not gain.
I will fight.

I hold on.
I cross the land.
I shall go on.
I will stand.

I grow weary.
I can not see.
I am the fury.
I will be.

I still stand.
I still fight.
I will not lose.
I will be right.

By
Josehf Lloyd Murchison

Dark Muse

Dark muse is about dark thought's dreams and reality.

The Faceless Woman was a ghost story told to me as a child. On fogy summer nights in the neighborhood where I grew up, we would retell the story of the faceless woman. I decided to make a poem of it.

The Curse of the Faceless Woman

Lost in time, this story is told, about a woman, dark and bold.
She walks the streets on a fogy night,
with a hood on her head to hide from sight.

Her story starts one summer's eve, beside a lake an evil deed.
A thief stole her daughter's life, and filled her soul with pain and strife.

On a moonlit night along the shore, two young lovers walked and more.
In each other's arms that night, they talked of love and held on tight.

In the morning they were found, their hands and feet with rope were bound.
Eyes wide open a vacant stare, their souls are gone and no ones there.

The police did search for the one, an evil deed to be undone.
In vain they search to no avail, their efforts weak, lost and pale.

A mother's heart broken and splayed, a debt to justice went unpaid.
She walked the streets at night alone, to make the sinners pay and atone.

She searched the shores by day and night, a vain attempt to make things right.
And then one early morning dawn, she was found her spirit gone.

On fogy night's times untold, she walks the streets dark and bold.
She only walks the streets at night, within the fog to hide her flight.

All clad in black she walks alone, an evil soul she'll make atone.
She walks among the starless night,
sometimes seen beneath the bright streetlight.

All children know to be aware, least they see her standing there.
They hurry home at the approach of night, sure that they would die at her sight.

So in the night if you should see, a woman in black, listen to me.
Look not at her face I say, Or with your soul you shall pay.

By
Josehf Lloyd Murchison

Mercy

Mercy has a fleeting heart,
to those that dare to see.
It does not know right from wrong,
it only knows pity.
To others it is shapeless,
never to be found.
For in the hearts of children,
to some it is abound.
It comes to those who need it most,
only when they die.
You see it in the hearts of man,
when they stop to cry.

By
Josehf Lloyd Murchison

A Child's Prayer

Beneath the covers he did lie.
With his head covered he did cry.
He begged the lord to let him die.
As tears would fall from his eye.

God please, please kill me this very night.
Please free me from this pain and terrible fright.
Please free me from this terror, anguish and sorrow.
Before I have to face tomorrow.

The lord did not answer a child's prayer.
He grew up believing no one did care.
Now he has an angry stare.
As there is a monster standing there.

By
Josehf Lloyd Murchison

Blind

My eyes are dim, I do not see.
How could this happen, to someone like me?
I'm not a bully, a thief or a cad.
Just a hard working man like my father and granddad.

As children we played a silly game.
Called blind mans bluff that was its name.
With our eyes covered, it's just not the same.
We remove the blindfold and we can see again.

Being blind is not like turning out the light.
The world is not dark as a moonless night.
Shades of gray without shape body or form.
To a blind man sight, this is the norm.

Why did this happen, to someone like me?
Was it God's way to teach me pity?
My eyes are dim, I cannot see.
Why did this happen, to someone like me?

By
Josehf Lloyd Murchison

Blessed Be

Blessed be the darkness.
For without the darkness, we would not know the light.
Born in darkness, the blind do not know the light.
To them the dark is the norm.

Born in the light, we see the sun, the moon and the stars.
We know the difference between the light and the dark.
If we lived in pleasure all our lives, we would not know it was pleasure.
It would just be.
But when we feel pain we learn the difference between pain and
pleasure.

We know that one we like and the other we don't.
In life we need the bad to teach us good is good.
That pain and sorrow hurt, and joy and life are pleasure.
Without death we would not crave life.

By
Josehf Lloyd Murchison

Aldorons Doom is in memory of a friend that died at the hands of the court.

Living with Schizophrenia he was harassed and tormented beyond endurance by the youth in the small town he lived until one day he drove off his tormentors at the point of a crossbow.

These misguided youth decided they had a right to tease my friend and in that belief called the Police claming they were attacked without provocation.

The Police bound by policy and ignorance, arrested my friend and held him over for trial. While in custody and without a comprehensive policy on the treatment of people in custody with mental health issues, he was denied his medication. It wasn't long and he became mentally unable to stand trial. Since he was mentally unable to stand trial he was released into the custody of his family for treatment.

On the way to the mental health institute, they stopped at their home to get a fresh change of clothing. He waited in the car as his father was in the house packing fresh clothing. His father was on the way back to the car when he heard the gunshot. My friend had taken his own life.

I never knew he lived with Schizophrenia, he never missed taking his medication. It was his medication that kept him stable enough to live a normal life. When he was denied his medication by the courts and custody, they may as well have shot him them selves.

Aldorons Doom

I stand upon the precipice of eternity,
before me certain doom.
My mind awash of misery,
all dark and filled with gloom.

The world a place of sorrow,
no man a mind of peace.
Life a burden of the sole,
its perils never cease.

I take a step into the void,
it does not end right there.
I hear the wind whistle,
as it passes through my hair.

The ground is growing closer,
I slowly close my eyes.
I feel the earth rising,
there will be no surprise.

By
Josehf Lloyd Murchison

Life's a Bitch

Times are hard and life's a bitch.
Sometimes your poor sometimes you're rich.
But don't be sad or in despair.
Suicide is always there.

By
Josehf Lloyd Murchison

Horror

Horror is born, this very day.
And with your soul, you shale pay.

Scream in horror and writhe in fear.
For I shale come and I am here.

I am vengeance, injustice and more.
I'll cut you up you fucking whore.

Your blood will run from my blade.
As your guts pore out your belly splayed.

I'll drink your blood from a goblet of glass.
As I bend you over and fuck your ass.

Scream in terror and writhe in pain.
For I shale rise to kill again.

By
Josehf Lloyd Murchison

Night Terrors

It sits hiding in the deep recesses of the mind, waiting in the dark for the moment when it can attack. Riding upon the winged beasts of the night, bringing horrors untold to those unaware of their intent.

Asleep and unable to defend one's self, night terrors attack. Seeking the young, the battered, the old, and the week, they breed and spread evil upon the world of the sleeping.

Feeding upon the screams in the minds of the unwary, these demons of the mind grow to consume all that is peaceful and serene. Savage and without mercy they tear apart all semblance of peace, in the dreams of there sleeping victims.

Riding the waves of the seas of our dreams as they are turned into unspeakable horrors of the mind, the dreamer finds their self at the bottom of the sea of sleep. With visions and horrors beyond telling all that is innocent and pure in the mind is beyond them, as the screams in the night feed the horror that torments their sleep.

Rest is futile as they thrash trying to throw off the demons that haunt their sleep never peaceful the night a thing of disembodied torment. They seek the death of sleep without dreams or flights of fancy, no children playing, no flowers blooming just the deep, dark, black, of a death like state.

Writhing in the agony of the images that haunt them, the dreamers are unable to free themselves from the terror that taunts, when freedom is only an awakening away.

By
Josehf Lloyd Murchison

The valley of dead souls

Jewel encrusted guardians of stone stand before the gates to the abyss of eternity. Above engraved in gilded stone inlaid with silver and gold are the words. Dearth of light and filled with gloom for all that enter seal their doom.

With deaths sweet kiss of nights never-ending silence to comfort them as they walk. Fires burn and give no warmth unto the abysmal souls that travel the path into the void. Pail from life drained drifting through eternity without regret for days long past. These lost souls marching on in their misery, no sunrise to inspire the eyes or sunset to charm the soul. Only pain to burden the flesh and dark sorrow to tire the sprit, as the fires of hell light the path.

This is the fate of souls devoid of a moral compass to guide them through life. Their sins guide them to the gates like a moth to a flame in the dark. In the wake of blood filled rivers of despair, innocent children cry tears of anguish upon the waters. Purity defiled by lust and greed feed the gluttony of their desires. Passion and love lost to indifference and hatred by the mindless desire to dominate the destitute and subjugated them to servitude.

All is lost to those that choose to walk this path to oblivion. None shall truly know the futility of wealth and power until they trudge this path of oblivion.

By
Josehf Lloyd Murchison

Footsteps in the snow

In the cold grip of winter's night it's the season of nature's rest. All is not at piece in this time of rest for the forest. All does not sleep.

The call of the Raven can be heard in the distance, as it echoes off the mountains to the forest below. Black capped chickadees and Titmice can be heard playing in the evergreens as sparkling gossamer snowflake's drift down from the heavens to the forest floor. Silently falling upon the trees and carpet of leaves at my feet to turn the forest white. Shimmering in the sun's light as if enchanted by the frost the forest comes to life. With gleaming crystals of ice the forest appears to animate in the suns embrace.

Without a breeze in the air the only sounds to be heard are my footsteps and the calls of birds. With the crunch of each step to keep me company, I walk along the path through the trees. As night approaches and the forest grows ever more quiet with each passing step. Gone are the calls of the forest's winter residents. All I hear are my footsteps in the snow as I walk. The life giving sun now below the horizon and no moon to light my way, I set light a torch to see the path.

In the dark the forest becomes a place of foreboding. The trees stand to the side like tombstones in a graveyard, the light from my torch dancing in the dark to create ominous shadows on the path. Like demons in the night they hide behind trees from the only witness to their gloomy presence.

In the dark the snow keeps falling in and out of my torchlight. The snow filled sky covers the moon and the stars hidden from my eyes in the night, I cannot track my progress as I trudge through the snow. The path grows deeper with each step I take my destination farther in the distance as I keep on walking through the cold and dark night hoping to see my destination. Wanting with each step to see the break in the trees that mark the open field to my home. I keep walking as if an eternity is passing searching for smallest glimmer of my cabin in the clearing. The snow crunching under my weight with each step I take. A dark foreboding chill runs down my spine and I look behind me, in the torchlight all I can see is footsteps in the snow.

By
Josehf Lloyd Murchison

Philosophy

There are times when the line between poetry and philosophy become blurred and this is why I included philosophy in Melodious Verse.

Everyone views death differently, in my case I don't view death as the end of life. Just as we are born we die and in time all that lives meet this fate in the circle of life.

Death

There is only one guarantee in life, death. From the first breath we take, to the last breath we expel. We walk with the angel of death. Death is beside us when we sleep. Death wakes with us each morning.

If we should falter as we walk through life, death is there to catch us when we fall. Freeing us from the burdens, pain and suffering, brought on by the prisons we create for ourselves.

Each person we touch we influence. Each person we influence we become a part of. When we touch another with words that we write, we influence them. Should what we write survive our demise, our ability to influence others survives.

For all intent and purposes, a part of us lives on forever in those we touch. We remain a part of the circle of life.

By
Josehf Lloyd Murchison

Circle of life

Each of all that exists on the earth has a circle in the web of life. Take a common stone for example. The stone forced up from the earth by the tectonic plates creates mountains. The mountains broken down by wind, rain and ice create boulders, rocks, and sand. These tumble down the mountain and into the rivers and valleys to create sand and soil. The sand and soil wash down the river to the ocean. In the ocean the sand and soil become compressed by the great pressures on the ocean floor, and return to stone.

How do stones fit in the web of life? The minerals from the stones feed the plants. The plants feed the animals. The animals feed the predators and the eaters of carrion. All live, reproduce, and die. All evacuate or biodegrade into the soil. The soil washes down the river to the ocean to become the stone. Each life interlocked with each other life on earth is dependent on each other.

We live in the circle of life; it starts at conception, and carries on throughout our lives. Some people are lucky enough to find love, reproduce and grow old. Others are not so lucky, they do not find love, or lost the one they love. Many others do not live long enough to find love or joy in life. All that lives ends in death and the circle of life is complete.

By
Josehf Lloyd Murchison

Enemy Mine

An enemy imagined is greater than an enemy that is real. For a real enemy can be killed, but an imagined enemy is invincible. No matter how much money we spend on defense, he will still exist. No matter how many we kill, the seed of its evil will spread. The true test of wisdom is to know the difference between an enemy imagined and an enemy that is real. To live in a world where peace is a dream and war is the norm, this is the reality of man. Our governments and corporations spend untold fortunes on the weapons and the technology of war. A great amount of our economy is based in the machines of war. Worst of all is the cost in the lives of our family, our friends and our neighbors.

In the small town where I live bombs do not fall, mines don't explode beneath our feet and children do not fall to sleep with the sound of gunfire. The night is not filled with fear and the cold. Their days are not filled with funerals, starvation and disease. Our children do not bury the dead or tend to the wounds of the injured. Long gone are the years of war with our neighbors and yet our children are still filled with the images and the horrors of war. Acts of terrorism abroad and at home fill the media with images of the dead and the dying. They haunt our minds with enemy's real and imagined that feed on paranoia and fear.

If an enemy did not exist those that need one would invent a cause to fight or an enemy to kill. Animal rights activists and others the like, use images of horror to rally people to their cause. A war suited to the needs of people dissatisfied with peace, activists create a political war to turn away from peace. If won they do not stop they push for vengeance against those that opposed them. Then in that act become an enemy of peace. Causes to be fought without complete victory they become a new group a hate group. They commit acts of violence against those that oppose them. They wave their criminal records like badges of honor. Without the concerns of peaceful resolution the exhilaration of violence beckons to them. Their cause a call to war.

By
Josehf Lloyd Murchison

Children

The greatest gift we give the future is our children.
We pay police to aid in the enforcement of our laws.
Not to shoot our children or us by accident.
Any fool can do that for free.

We train police to do a job and we arm them to protect us,
not to shoot us by mistake or to imprison the innocent.
And yet they do.

If they continue to commit these crimes against the people,
maybe it is time to reconsider hiring them.

By
Josehf Lloyd Murchison

Freedom

Freedom isn't free it is paid for in blood sweat and the lives of the people willing to give there lives for what they believe in. Soldiers, Warriors, Writers, Poets and Freedom fighters all give their lives, blood, words and future to the cause of freedom. With the hopes that the future will give life to their dreams of justice without tyranny they give all that they will be to the call of freedom.

Will their sacrifice be remembered or forgotten to the winds of time like the leaves in a tree come the winter. Forgotten are the reasons for laws to protect the rights of the individual and replaced with laws that give power to a few of little scruples. Activists with their hearts in vengeance or politically correct hate that band together to oppress those that offend them. Corporations that take advantage of the indifference of politicians and the courts to control and profit from the masses that feed their desire for power.

Freedom isn't lost in one felled swoop it is lost one law at a time. With amendments to the constitution the rights of all grow smaller until they no longer exist. With each new law built upon the amendments freedom is lost to everyone and the sacrifices of the ones that gave their lives and their futures to the call of freedom is lost and forgotten to indifference. Is this what they gave their life, their blood and their future for? To be forgotten, ignored and lost to time.

It is up to us to remember the sacrifices of our forefathers and even the people they fought against. To read the poems written to the bravery of the ones that gave their future. To sing the songs of the heroes and the villains. To remember the stories of the survivors and the fallen in the battle for freedom. To carry on the fight for freedom and remember the sacrifices, pain and sorrow. If we do not remember, if we do not carry on the fight for freedom. We will be lost to the prisons of our own construction and their dreams, their futures and their sacrifices will have been in vain.

By
Josehf Lloyd Murchison

Good

A tool forged of the purest heart becomes an instrument of evil in the hands of a blackguard. All that is good is only good if in the hand of the pure of heart. However should evil lurk within the heart of the holder then evil is the tool.

Just because you can, does that mean you should? This is a question that many engineers and scientists seldom ask themselves as they build, design or create. Once they have created a device they cannot control whose hands hold that device. Once they develop a theory and don't think about how what they create will be used who is responsible for how it is used? If Einstein considered the possibility that his theory would be used to make a weapon would he have made it public? Did he know? Did he care beforehand? Did the scientists that built the bomb think about the children killed, wounded and maimed for life? They knew its use. Whatever the reason the death of innocent children can never be justified.

The lasers first intent was a weapon of war but it did not work as a weapon. The closest to weaponry use today is guidance systems. Used as a medical tool or a measuring device sometimes the weapon becomes a tool for good. This is not to be forever as scientists and engineers are still today trying to make the weapon work.

If you were one of the people working on this weapon would you make it work?

Would you find a new job?

Would you think about the children, the mothers, the fathers, the brothers and the sisters?

Would you say if I don't build it someone else will and line your pockets with the blood of others?

Or would you think?

The law is a tool of justice so I ask to whom does the heart belong?

By
Josehf Lloyd Murchison

JUSTICE

Justice is not justice without mercy and mercy is not mercy without justice. For without justice no matter how merciful a punishment it is cruel and unusual punishment to an innocent person. Vengeance is not justice for to have justice you must have mercy and vengeance is without mercy. Vengeance cares not for rehabilitation or forgiveness.

Vengeance has its heart in the pursuit of inflicting pain and suffering upon those that offend them and not in justice or mercy.

There is an old saying amongst aboriginal north Americans, "Vengeance is a dish best served cold."

There is nothing colder than a dead heart freed from the constraints of a conscience. Without the forethought to consider the repercussions of their actions they act without a thought as to the ramifications to others. The pain they inflict on their offender does not end at their offender. The pain carries on to all that witness the act or the aftermath.

Do you think a child sees his father as a villain or a hero? Do they see their mother as a witch or an angel? When you exact revenge on that person do you harm the offender or the child? Does a vendetta undo the evil that was done or does it make it grow and give it a life of its own?

Injustice gives evil a place to grow and a mind to destroy.

By
Josehf Lloyd Murchison

Mercy's Chance

Show mercy to the merciful and it my be returned.
Show mercy to the merciless and it will not be returned.

The merciless would not show mercy to you.
The merciless would use mercy to trap you and all that you hold dear.

The merciless has no heart or conscience, in it is only an abyss.
Kindness is lost on an empty heart.

By
Josehf Lloyd Murchison.

Our Charge

I hunt, fish and gather from the forest the food for my table. Unlike city people who only see the meat on the store shelf, I see the life sacrificed to nourish my family. It never ceases to amaze me, the number of people whom I meet each day that never considers the lives of the creatures that feed their family.

I butcher the meat and I raise and gather the vegetables my on my table. I see the lamb born, grow and graze upon the meadow. My children learn to respect the creatures that feed them. They learn to care for all that they are in charge of.

When I was a boy, the whole family would go to the stream each spring. We would fish for smelt in the early evening. Later that night, we would clean and freeze the smelt. In the summer I would catch tadpoles, frogs and turtles. Sometimes I went fishing in that stream.

Other times I just sat on the bank of that stream and watched the creatures that lived there.

Today that stream is no more than a drainage ditch. There are no more turtles, fish or frogs. All the wild plants, and flowers are gone. All the life stripped from the stream by developers, landowners and the like. Dead and barren like a wasteland in a drought, nothing lives there but the most rugged of small creatures. Lost to time and greed.

If people do not take the time to save the creatures in the world there will never be any for our children to enjoy. The farms and fields that surrounded the town I lived in are all gone now replaced by factories and office buildings. The pheasant, the groundhogs and the rabbits have left for wild spaces unknown. The creatures of the night have fled in the dark and all is quiet now. Little survives the onslaught of man and little will be left if we continue to be the destroyer.

By
Josehf Lloyd Murchison

Erotica and the Pen

Erotica is one of the most difficult subjects to write. Good stories and poetry have sex violence and suspense. This article is on writing about sex without profanities.

When you write a story or a poem, where two people make love you have a choice about how it is written. Unless your readers are into profanities you risk loosing readers that are offended by profanities.

The last thing a writer wants to do is ostracize their readers. It's not the same as a humorous limerick like, "There once was a man from Nantucket." or a character in a novel saying, "Fuck you and the horse you rode in on." In humor or a limerick the readership expects profanity. In novels readers expect the bad guys to swear. However many readers expect the hero to be pure, even while making love.

We expect our heroes to say, "We made passionate love all night long." not, "I fucked the ass off her." A scum bag biker would say, "She sucked my cock until I came in her mouth and she swallowed my gizzum." Our hero would say, "The touch of her lips on my skin sent waves of pleasure through every ounce of my being, until I could contain my self no more."

As much as clinical terminology are not profanities they are not passionate. You can call a man's penis a phallus, a cock or you can call it his manhood. A writer could write, "He pleased me as he shoved his penis in my vagina." or a writer could say, "He pleasured me with every thrust in me." Here I have portrayed the same message with out mentioning the body parts involved. The only clinical term I have ever herd that retains its beauty and passion is breast. "Tears of joy ran down her face as she held her child to her breast." Or "She held his body to her breast as he lay sleeping."

When a writer writes a story, poem or any form of art, they must consider their readers and how they want there readers to perceive them. Do you want your readers to perceive you as a Gangster Rapper or a sensitive passionate writer? The choice is yours, pick one you can live with.

By
Josehf Lloyd Murchison

Humor

Every piece a writer writes doesn't need to be deep or dark, a little humor goes a long way to bringing joy into your life when you can find it.

His right hand

His right hand is his lover;
to it he will be true.
For if it weren't for fingers,
he always would be blue.

His right hand is his lover;
he plays each and every night.
He pulls, and pulls with rhythm.
Stroking with all his might.

His right hand is his lover;
and when he wants a gas.
He greases up a finger,
and slides it up his ass.

By
Josehf Lloyd Murchison

Critiques

Critiques are not to stroke like a phallus.
Nor are they to be in anger or malice.
If ones structure points to a technique.
Then that's what must be in your critique.
Whether Waka, Tie or Haiku.
Only the rules in these will do.

Not every one will like what you write.
So don't consider critiques a slight.
If you don't understand what I say.
To this next part, attention do pay.
Perfect in structure shape and form.
For Tie poetry this is the norm.

Tie Poetry

Tie poetry has three rules.
1. Each word must be one on. (Syllable)
2. There are only two lines in the Tie poem.
3. And there are only three words in a line.
With that in mind this is a Tie poem.

Up your but.
You numb nut.

By
Josehf Lloyd Murchison

I Hit Your Car

I hit your car in the parking lot.
I was there and you were not.
So I write this note as the people watch,
and my licence plate they will botch.
And now this driver he must go.
I don't want to be here when you show.

By
Josehf Lloyd Murchison

My Darling Dear

On a business trip up north I hit a deer with my car. Since in Ontario you can keep road kill I dropped the deer off at a local butcher and continued on my trip. On the way back from my business I picked up the venison from the butcher and brought it home.

My wife was preparing a roast of venison for supper and I asked her not to tell our two children what the roast was, If they asked I would give them a hint.

When supper was served I told the children we were eating something special for dinner. They recognized the potatoes and vegetables right away when my son asked, "What kind of meat is this daddy?"

When I told him that it was something mommy calls daddy. My daughter yelled, "Don't eat it Billy it's an ass hole."

By
Josehf Lloyd Murchison

Jerky

Years ago in a small town I worked in a feed mill. One of my co- workers had a donkey that broke its leg. Not wanting it to go to waste he shot the donkey and had it butchered for meat.

When the butcher was finished preparing the meat, he brought some of the Jerky to work for us to try.

After a couple of old time farmers and I tasted a portion of the Jerky we thanked Brad for, THE PIECE OF ASS.

By
Josehf Lloyd Murchison

Pork Chop

I was driving a big rig on State highway 59 in Texas when I stopped at a truck stop in Shepherd Texas for fuel. After I paid for the fuel I returned to my truck by walking through the drivers lounge.

The truck drivers on downtime were watching a program on sex in the lounge as I walked through. The lady speaking on the program said, "The average male ejaculate has the same amount of protein as a pork chop."

At that point I perked up and said, "No wonder my wife is so fat."

I could hear the other truckers laughing as I carried on to my truck.

By
Josehf Lloyd Murchison

Monica Lewinsky

There is a new school in the south called The Monica Lewinsky School of Business, where our motto is you get a head by giving.

We have Richard Simmons as the dean of physical education.

And Bill Clinton as the dean of Political Sciences specializing in oral exams.

Michael Jackson gave up the seat, as Dean of the Music Department to PeeWee Herman sighting the student body was to mature for his curriculum.

And Jason Vorheas is dean of self-defense and summer school.

By
Josehf Lloyd Murchison

Writing

At first it may appear simple to write a poem or a story in truth it isn't. I read every thing I come across. Autopsy reports, Inquests reports, witness statements, news articles, I have even read encyclopaedia sets. First it expands your vocabulary and your knowledge of history; which is very valuable it also provides inspiration.

One inspiration my experiences have given me is, "Justice is not justice with out mercy. And mercy is not mercy without justice, for without justice no mater how merciful a punishment it is cruel and unjust punishment to an innocent man."

Several innocent men whom spent ten and more years in prison for crimes they not only didn't commit, in several cases the crime never happen inspired "Justice."

Inspiration can be found in the most unlikely places, a bus, and parks or while fishing on a lake. I have taken to carrying a tape recorder so that when a thought strikes me I can record it and visit it at a later time when I have the time to work on it. I have at times put several different thoughts recorded at different times together to make one piece. Don't be afraid to work a piece, or to just walk away from it and then to come back to it at a later date. Don't just look at things see them, when you read create an image of what you read in your mind. When you write create an image with your words the clearer the image in your mind the clearer the image in a readers minds. Most importantly don't write above the ability of your readerships ability to comprehend. If your readers cannot understand what you have written, your writing is lost on them and will not inspire.

Getting started; keep it simple, make notes, visualize, work the piece and rework the piece. If you get stuck take a break and come back to it later with a fresh mind. Read everything and most of all live and experience life the greatest inspiration of all.

By
Josehf Lloyd Murchison

Table of Contents